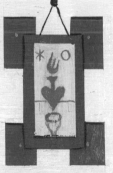

For my beloved nephew August. —M.B.

*For Sophie Ella Rogers, may you continue to be
inspired through wide-eyed curiosity, goodness, and joy,
with all the love and blessings from your family.* —J.P.

First published in the United States, Great Britain, Canada, Australia, and New Zealand in 2017
by NorthSouth Books, Inc., an imprint of NordSüd Verlag AG, CH-8050 Zürich, Switzerland.

Distributed in the United States by NorthSouth Books, Inc., New York 10016.
Library of Congress Cataloging-in-Publication Data is available.
ISBN: 978-0-7358-4269-4
Printed in Germany 2017
1 3 5 7 9 • 10 8 6 4 2
www.northsouth.com

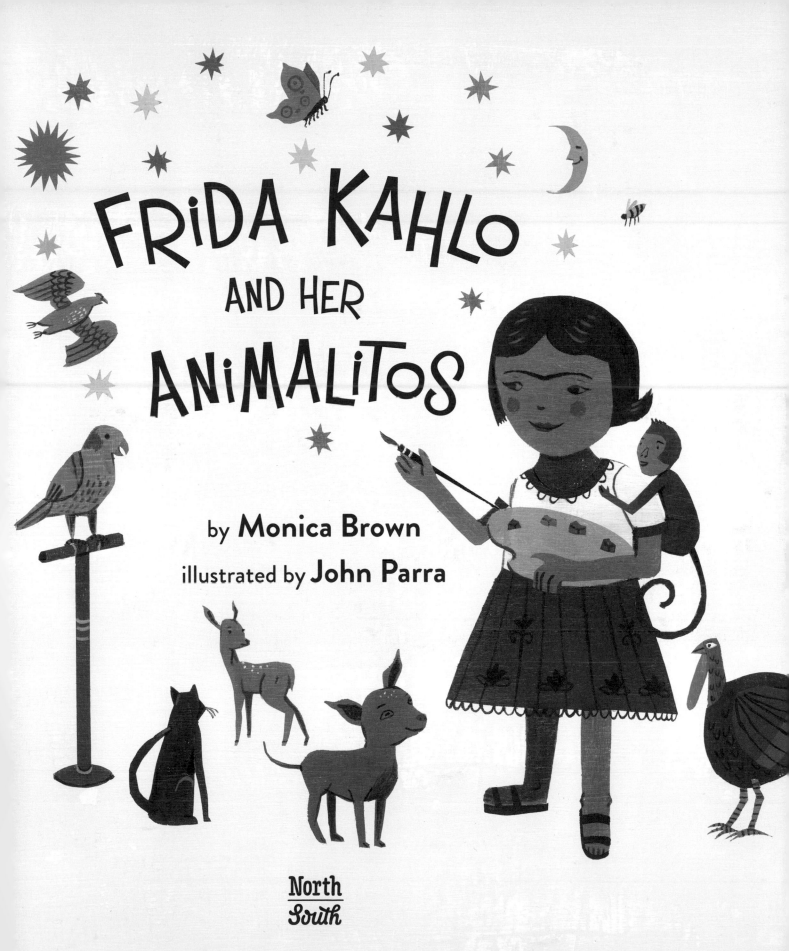

FRIDA KAHLO
AND HER
ANiMALiTOS

by **Monica Brown**

illustrated by **John Parra**

North South

This is the story of a little girl named Frida who grew up to be one of the most famous painters of all time. Frida was special.

This is also the story of two monkeys, a parrot, three dogs, two turkeys, an eagle, a black cat, and a fawn. They were Frida's pets, and they were special too.

Frida had a parrot named Bonito.
Like her parrot, Frida was colorful.
She liked to wear bold shades that
celebrated indigenous Mexico and her

own heritage. She lived in a house the color of a parrot's bright-blue feather— La Casa Azul—where she grew up with her mom, dad, and sisters.

Frida had a pet fawn named Granizo. Like her fawn, Frida had watchful, beautiful eyes. When Frida closed her eyes, she remembered her life as a little girl.

Frida was always with her father, a photographer who taught her to look at the world through curious eyes. Frida and her father would walk to the park to collect bugs to look at under a microscope. Frida's father also taught her how to paint finishing touches on his photographs. Frida loved the small brushes and the beautiful colors.

Frida had a cat with black, shiny fur, the same color as her long dark hair. Like a cat, Frida was playful. But as a child, Frida couldn't always play.

When Frida was six, she got very sick. She was in bed for a long time. But little Frida didn't get sad or bored. Instead, she used her breath to make mist on her window, and then she drew a door with her finger. Frida used her big imagination and curious eyes to walk out the door with a magic friend—a little girl who danced and played like a kitten!

Frida was independent, like a cat! Frida's sickness left one of her legs different from the other and children made fun of her, but this didn't stop Frida from skating and riding bikes and rowing on the lakes of Chapultepec Park so that her leg could get stronger. Frida was not afraid to do things other little girls didn't usually do—she wore overalls and boxed and wrestled!

Frida had two spider monkeys—Fulang Chang and Caimito del Guayabal. Like her monkeys, Frida could be mischievous, even when she was a teenager!

When Frida was fifteen, she went to a school called the Preparatoria, and found a group of friends she loved.

Like Frida, her friends were curious to learn all they could. Together they read and studied and argued and sometimes got in trouble! Wearing matching caps, they rode donkeys through halls of the Preparatoria and set off firecrackers.

Frida had an eagle named Gertrudis. Like her eagle, Frida's imagination could fly high.

When Frida was eighteen she was in a terrible accident and once again she had to be in bed for many months. This time Frida didn't create a magic friend— she created art! Frida's mother made her a special easel and hung a mirror over her canopy bed so Frida could paint. Frida used her imagination and curious eyes to do just that.

"Feet, what do I need you for when I have wings to fly?"

And if those weren't enough pets, Frida had two turkeys and three dogs—Señor Xolotl, Señorita Capulina, and Señora Kosti!

Frida's turkeys were intelligent and sensitive, just like herself. And, like Frida, her dogs were warm and loving. When she was lonely or sad, she would wrap her arms around them and they would comfort her.

Her Xolo dogs were the same breed that ran and hunted with the Aztecs thousands of years ago—and a reflection of Frida's heritage of which she was very proud! Frida's dogs had no hair, but their bodies were warm, and Frida gave them great big hugs whenever she felt lonely or sad.

Frida's *animalitos* were spirited and entertaining, just like Frida.

When her two spider monkeys were being good, Frida would hold them like babies. When they were being mischievous, they would steal socks and fruit and leap through windows so no one could catch them!

Her parrot named Bonito liked to snuggle under the covers while Frida took naps and would do tricks at the dinner table for pats of butter.

Frida's animalitos played all day in the courtyard at La Casa Azul, the bright-blue house on Londres Street. Her husband, Diego Rivera, even made the animals a pyramid to climb on so that her pets could roam freely!

When Frida painted, her pets would keep her company. And Frida painted all the time, while the birds sang, the dogs barked, and the turkeys danced in the garden.

Frida's animals were her children, her friends, and her inspiration.

Frida painted when she was sick and hurting, and Frida painted when she was happy. She also painted when Diego was gone and she was sad. But Frida was never really alone at La Casa Azul, the bright-blue house on Londres Street. She had her animalitos and herself, and she painted both.

Frida painted herself with Fulang Chang
playing with ribbons. She painted herself
with Bonito the parrot and Señor Xolotl the
dog. She painted her black cat too, peeking
over her shoulder.

Frida painted herself with all the pets she loved so much—and even butterflies and caterpillars. Her paintings were magic.

And today, if you visit La Casa Azul in Coyoacán, just outside of Mexico City, you might hear the sound of a bird, or see a black cat jump from the pyramid that sits in the courtyard of the bright-blue house on Londres Street where Frida and her animalitos lived so many years ago.

MUSEO
FRIDA KAHLO

AUTHOR'S NOTE

Magdalena Carmen Frieda Kahlo y Calderón, otherwise known as Frida Kahlo, was born in 1907 at 247 Londres Street in the city of Coyoacán, which means place of Coyotes in Náhuatl, the language of the Aztecs. Frida, as she came to be called, was the daughter of a mestiza Mexican mother and a German Hungarian father.

Frida's life was marked by many things, and among them was illness. When Frida was only six, she contracted polio; and in 1925, when she was eighteen, she was in a terrible bus accident that left her with pain and health problems throughout her life. It was during the long months when she was bedridden that she took up painting seriously, and her subject was most often the face in the mirror—herself. She also painted her animals, who were her constant companions throughout her adult life.

I've always been intrigued by Frida's relationship to her animal companions. Although Frida didn't get her most famous pets until she was an adult, I chose to write about Frida's animalitos as a way of highlighting Frida's magical creativity—her strength, her sense of adventure, her indomitable spirit—throughout her life. What insights do her beloved animals tell us about the young Frida? It was an honor to use *lo real maravilloso* (the marvelous real) to imagine just that.

Fulang, Caimito del Guayabal, Bonito, Señor Xolotl, Señorita Capulina, and Señora Kosti were some of Frida's many pets. There was also Granizo the fawn, Gertrudis "Caca Blanca" the eagle, two turkeys, peacocks, two more cats (Galletacera and Tomic), and other dogs (Sombra, Kaganovich, Alfa, and Beta) that played in the courtyard at La Casa Azul. As a young artist, Frida shared her paintings with one of Mexico's most famous muralists, Diego Rivera. Diego thought she was gifted and enchanting. Eventually Diego and Frida married, and their partnership changed contemporary Mexican art forever.

Frida's paintings have hung in the Louvre and Musée de l'Orangerie in Paris, the Metropolitan Museum of Art in New York City, and major galleries all over the world—Mexico, the United States, England, Sweden, Germany, Canada, and Japan. In 2001, Frida was the first Latina to be honored with a US postage stamp. Frida was a brilliant painter; and her self-portraits offer insight into a passionate, pain-, and love-filled life. Frida couldn't have children, but she surrounded herself with people she loved and her many pets. Of Frida's paintings, more than fifty are self-portraits, and in many she depicts herself with her animalitos. They kept her company, amused her, and brought her comfort. You can see some of Frida's pets in the following selection of paintings:

Fulang-Chang and I, 1937
Xoloitzcuintle-Dog with Me, 1938
Self-Portrait with Monkey and Ribbon on the Neck, 1940
Self-Portrait with Bonito, 1941
Me and My Parrots, 1941
Self-Portrait with Monkey and Parrot, 1942
Self-Portrait with Monkeys, 1943
Self-Portrait with Monkey, 1945
Self-Portrait with Monkey [and Señor Xolotl], 1945
Still Life with Parrot and Flag, 1951
*Self Portrait with a Portrait of Diego on the Breast
 and Maria Between the Eyebrows*, 1954

Between 1926 and 1954, Frida Kahlo painted more than two hundred paintings, each one a gift to the future. Her work has inspired future generations of artists, and anyone who opens his or her mind to the brilliance of her curious eyes. Her art is also a gift to all who struggle with illness in silence. Frida used her paintbrush to create beauty from pain, and to find strength in the midst of suffering.

"Frida Kahlo with Fulang Chang" by Florence Arquin
from the series Frida Kahlo: Her Photos
(Courtesy Museos Frida Kahlo y Diego Rivera-Anahuacalli)